This book is dedicated to my students
past, present and future.

You give me so much joy!
Thank you!

CONTENTS

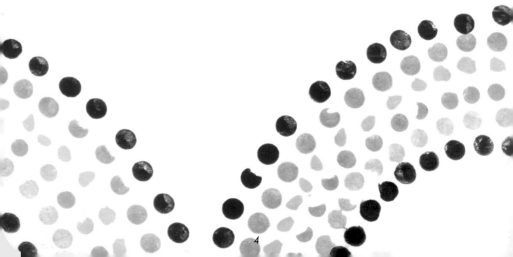

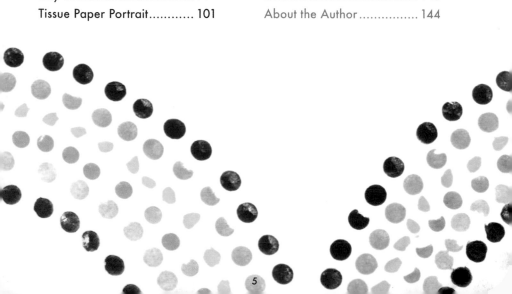

INTRODUCTION

When I was young I was given a few books and magazines that were geared towards making things – mostly on your own without having to ask an adult for help. Often they didn't have patterns to work from and they used simple materials to make the projects. These books seemed like magic to me! They made me think of possibilities. I loved to dream up my own variations on the projects. My parents were supportive and provided me with a small sized table and area where I could make and paint and construct for a whole afternoon, if I wanted to – which I often did! I hope this book inspires you to make and paint and create, too!

HOW TO USE THIS BOOK

Art Camp is a collection of fifty-two projects made from simple materials. They are open ended projects that promote creativity and confidence in art making. The projects can be done with little or no supervision for most elementary school aged children. The children will gain confidence and skill building with each lesson.

Common sense should be exercised when using sharp scissors and sewing needles and we suggest supervision where the adult in charge deems it to be necessary.

Learning to thread a needle and use it properly is one of the most empowering lessons I have taught in my own classrooms to both children and adults. Simple stitches are also the basis of many fine art objects and most kids are excited to learn this skill. Some of the book's projects will create toys to play with and others will make art to admire.

These lessons were designed to be enjoyed by both children and adults – as it's never too late to create something wonderful!

LET'S GET STARTED

Setting up a space to work can be as simple as a small folding table and chair. It's nice to have a dedicated spot to make art and yet it's easy to create these projects at the kitchen table too! A sturdy surface and good light to work by is essential. Some projects could even be made outside, weather permitting. Each lesson has a small list of items needed to create the project. Gather materials before you start to focus on art making. Cover your work area with newspaper or a plastic tablecloth that you can wipe down. Protect your clothes with an apron or old oversized tee shirt. These simple preparations make it easy to enjoy creating.

The materials list covers the basic materials you can have on hand to make everything in the book. I also have included the recipes to make the exceptional air dry clay (made from two ingredients!) and paste paper paints that we use in our own studios. These are found on page 142.

Finally, in the back of the book I have curated a small gallery of artists who work in less traditional ways . I find them fascinating and hope you enjoy meeting them and learning about their work.

MATERIALS LIST

This list is a reference for all the projects in the book. You don't need everything all at once! Gather them slowly and store them in recycled jars, small labeled boxes and cans to have them ready for creating!

- Scissors small and large
- Pencils with erasers
- Crayons - remove paper
- Acrylic craft paints – assorted colors in small bottles
- Paintbrushes – soft and bristle types
- Clear Elmers glue
- UHU glue stick – because it works!
- Low melt hot glue – supervised by an adult!
- Glitter
- Non-drying modeling clay
- Copy paper
- Watercolor paper – inexpensive pads student grade
- Cover stock – from office supply stores
- Newspaper – plenty of it!
- Tissue paper – assorted colors
- Old magazines and discarded books
- Colored papers – origami, construction
- Skewers
- Masking tape
- Cardboard – recycled cereal boxes, corrugated and thin packaging style
- Markers – washable, fine point and permanent
- Pens – ballpoint and gel
- Sticks – driftwood or backyard
- Stones smooth, small and round
- Pinecones, moss, leaves
- Recycled bubble wrap
- Coffee cans and small recycled jars with lids
- String - embroidery floss, waxed linen cord and cotton string
- Toothpicks
- Recycled paper- tubes, boxes, junk mail, graph paper, empty matchboxes
- Felt and yarn
- Scrap wood and wooden embroidery hoops
- Styrofoam balls
- Liquid starch
- Paper clips and rubber bands
- Dowels, chopsticks
- Paper and foam plates
- Waxed paper

What you'll need:
· Cardboard tube
· Craft acrylic paint
· Small paint brush
· Pipe cleaner
· Scissors
· Clear glue

LET'S MAKE ART!

1. Cut a paper tube into sections. Fold down one end to make "ears". Paint the cat all over with one color and let dry.

2. When dry choose another color for stripes or spots or calico cat markings. It's your choice!

3. Paint on the eyes, ears, nose and mouth if you like. Let dry.

4. Cut a pipe cleaner in half, then bend in half to make whiskers. Glue in place and let dry. Give the cats a ball of yarn to play with!

What you'll need:

· Tissue paper in assorted colors
· Small spray bottle with water
· Heavyweight paper

LET'S MAKE ART!

1. Tear the tissue paper into small shapes.

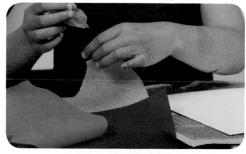

2. Place the pieces on the heavyweight paper.

3. Spray them with the water and let them dry for a few minutes.

4. Pull off the tissue paper and see what you have painted. Continue with more paper.

HINT: You can try cutting the paper into shapes too!

What you'll need:
· Set of watercolors
· Bristle paintbrush
· Plastic needlepoint canvas
· Thick paper
· Container of water

LET'S MAKE ART!

1. Spread out newspaper. Place the heavy paper on top.

2. Wet your brush first, then dry it a bit by brushing it back and forth on the newspaper. Choose a color and brush it with your brush until the bristles are full of paint.

3. Place the plastic needlepoint canvas on the paper. Bounce the brush up and down through the holes of the canvas until the paint is gone. Change colors and keep repeating step 2.

4. Move the canvas around the paper until you fill the space up as you like!

What you'll need:

· Heavyweight paper
· Watercolor set
· Soft paintbrush
· Container of water
· Pencil
· Finepoint marker

VILLAGE TRIPTYCH

LET'S MAKE ART!

1. Use a paper that is twice as wide as it is high. Fold both ends to meet in the center to create three panels.

2. Draw lightly first with a pencil, a village scene. This can be inspired by where you live, a place in a story or an imaginary village.

3. Use the watercolor to add color to the drawing. To keep colors from running into each other - remember to let wet areas dry before adding more color next to it.

4. When dry – add details with the fine point marker.

What you'll need:
· Ink pads
· Pencils with new erasers
· Paper

LET'S MAKE ART!

1. Fold the paper in half to make a card. Press the pencil eraser into the ink pad.

2. Press the eraser onto the paper to make a dot. A lot of dots in a row make a line!

3. Get plenty of ink by re-inking each time and pressing hard on the card! Use a different pencil eraser for each color.

4. Create your own patterns and images using one or more colors. Write words with dots! Create a card for any occasion.

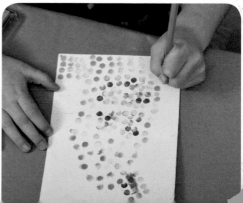

What you'll need:

· A thumb!
· Ink pads
· Paper
· Fineline marker

LET'S MAKE ART!

1. Press your thumb into one ink color. Print the flower petals first.

2. Use a finger to create a center for the flower with a different ink color. Make a stem from a line of fingerprints.

3. Add clouds and sky and raindrops with your thumb.

4. Add details with the fineline marker, if you want. Our artist chose to outline his objects.

HINT: Get Ed Emberley's books on making more art with thumbprints!

What you'll need:

· Leaves
· Craft Acrylic Paints
· Newspaper to protect workspace
· Bristle brush
· Paper plate
· Paper

LET'S MAKE ART!

1. Dispense the paint on the paper plate. Paint the back of one leaf with one or more colors.

2. Take the paper and carefully place it over the wet painted leaf. Press hard without moving the paper.

3. Lift up the paper to see your print!

HINT: Try using just black paint on white paper. Let dry and color in with markers or crayons!

4. Decide on the next color and repeat the process. You can overlap prints and try different shaped leaves. Always paint the backside of the leaf as the veins are most raised there and will give you the best print!

23

What you'll need:

· Graph paper
· Markers
· Scissors
· UHU glue stick
· Black paper

LET'S MAKE ART!

1. Draw a variety of objects (flowers, robots, animals, faces) using the squares in the paper as a guide. Fill in the squares and "build" your objects by connecting the squares.

2. Cut out your objects following the squares. Arrange them on the black paper.

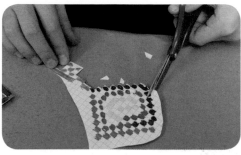

3. Put glue on the back of each object working from the center out to the edges.

4. Press them firmly onto the black paper.

What you'll need:

- · Short cardboard tube
- · Pencil
- · Black marker
- · Acrylic craft paints
- · Soft brush
- · Paper plate
- · Newspaper to protect workspace

LET'S MAKE ART!

1. Draw an oval with the pencil in the middle of the tube as shown. Paint around the tube as you like, leaving the oval blank until the end. Paint it white or another color you choose!

2. Using the black marker draw the face of the person who is going to receive the gift box. Make a decorative edge around the edge of the oval, if desired.

3. Fold in one side of the tube. Fold in the opposite side to close the bottom of the box.

4. Fill with small candies, a tiny gift or a tiny card you made. Fold the top sides down to seal. Give the gift away!

What you'll need:

- · Paper plates
- · Bubble wrap
- · Acrylic craft paint
- · Newspaper to protect workspace
- · Foam brush
- · Scissors

LET'S MAKE ART!

1. Cut the paper plate into a spiral from the outside edge to the center of the plate as shown.

2. Brush the paint onto the piece of bubble wrap to cover.

3. Press the bubble wrap onto the spiral-cut paper plate to print. Use large and small bubble wrap for printing. Continue with other colors on both sides to cover.

4. Tie with a string and hang where there is a breeze. Watch them spin!

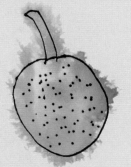

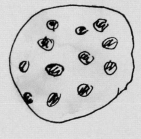

What you'll need:

· Watercolor paper
· Watercolor set
· Spray bottle of water
· Soft brush
· Water
· Fine point marker
· Newspaper to protect work area

LET'S MAKE ART!

1. Spray the watercolor paper in one area with water.

2. With a wet brush, choose a color of paint for your first blot. Use a lot of paint! Touch the brush gently to the water on the paper. Watch it spread.

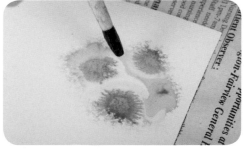

3. Try another area and repeat the process until all of the space on the paper is used up. Let dry.

4. Look at your blots and dots – what do you see? Using the fine point marker, draw details into the blots and dots to bring what you see to life!

What you'll need:

· Black paper
· White colored pencil
· Masking tape
· Scissors
· Pencils or straws

LET'S MAKE ART!

1. Think of an animal or group of animals to draw. Draw them on the black paper with a white colored pencil. Make them big enough to fit over the end of a pencil or straw. We chose a shark with three fish.

2. Cut out the animals.

3. Tape them to the pencils or straws securely on the back side of the paper.

4. Make up a story to tell with your puppets. Make a theater by tacking a sheet across a doorway and putting a lamp without a shade behind the sheet. Hold your puppets between the lamp and the backside of the sheet so your audience sees the shadow from your puppets!

What you'll need:

· Metal can
· Bubble wrap and tape
· Large piece of paper (recycled paper bags cut open and flattened work great!)
· Assorted acrylic craft paints
· Paper plate
· Foam brush

LET'S MAKE ART!

1. Tape the bubble wrap around the can.

2. Stand the can upright and brush the paint onto the bubble wrap.

3. Roll the can back and forth and across the paper to print.

4. Repeat with as many colors as you want to use. You can cover the can with different sized bubble wrap to get different sized prints.

What you'll need:

· Discarded compact disc
· Assorted colors of ink pads
· Pencils with new eraser ends
· Paper

LET'S MAKE ART!

1. Place the CD on your paper. Choose a color and press your eraser into it. Press the eraser onto the paper at the outside edge of the CD. Continue by re-inking the eraser and printing around the CD. Remove the CD.

2. Choose another color of ink and follow around the first circle of dots you made.

3. Keep going with new colors of ink making a rainbow of colors around your first circle.

4. Add other circles in the corner or elsewhere on the paper. Let them go off the page and be only partially on the paper.

What you'll need:

· Paper tube
· Waxed paper
· Rubber band
· Acrylic craft paints
· Soft paint brush
· Water
· Newspaper to protect work area

LET'S MAKE ART!

1. Choose the colors to paint the paper tube. Paint around it in stripes as we did, or choose another pattern.

2. Cover the tube with paint completely. Let dry.

3. Cover one end with a square of waxed paper.

4. Secure the waxed paper with the rubber band. Play your kazoo by humming loudly into it. It will make a fun buzzing sound! Try playing along with your favorite songs on the radio.

What you'll need:

· Old magazines
· Cereal box flattened and cut up
· Pencil
· Scissors
· UHU glue stick

LET'S MAKE ART!

1. Look through the magazines to find photos of people which show their full body from head to toe. Cut out the page first, then cut out the person.

2. Glue the cutout onto the front side of the cereal box. Press hard to make it stick well. The lightweight cardboard of the box will help your person stand up.

3. Cut out the cardboard around the edges of the photo, but leave a wider part of the cardboard to the left and right of the feet.

4. To make a base, cut out a half circle a little wider than the paper doll's shoulders. Cut one slit from the top in the middle of the half circle and one slit in the center of the bottom of the paper doll. Join the two pieces in the shape of a cross to stand the doll up!

HINT: Make paper pets for your dolls! Make up stories for the dolls to act out.

What you'll need:

· Materials
· Old magazines
· Paper
· Scissors
· UHU glue stick

CRAZY COLLAGE PEOPLE

LET'S MAKE ART!

1. Look through old magazines to find photos of people. Cut out their heads, torsos, legs, arms, feet and hands. Mix them up – changing heads and other parts.

2. Look for a background for the people to be part of. Cut out the background. Arrange on the paper to fit behind the person.

3. Apply glue to the background first and stick it to your paper.

4. Assemble your crazy collage person by gluing down one piece at a time on top of the background.

HINT: Make a group of crazy collage people together!

What you'll need:

- Small cardboard rectangles
- Rubber bands
- Clear glue
- Paper clips
- Old file folders cut into shapes
- Scissors
- White and black paper
- Crayons
- UHU glue sticks

LET'S MAKE ART!

1. On one piece of cardboard put drops of glue in a pattern. On another cardboard, glue down paper clips with the clear glue. On another glue down shapes you cut from the file folders. On another glue down some toothpicks. On the last one wrap rubber bands around the cardboard and secure with clear glue. Let dry overnight.

2. Cover the texture plates with a piece of white paper. Rub as shown with the side of a crayon. Turn the plates for a different effect. Try different crayon colors too. Your papers now have visual texture!

3. Cut out shapes from your texture papers to make a robot or made-up creature. Use different papers for the different parts.

4. Lay out the pieces on the black paper and glue them down.

What you'll need:

- Assortment of sticks
- Tacky glue
- Scrap wood base
- Assorted craft acrylic paints
- Water
- Soft tiny brush

LET'S MAKE ART!

1. Arrange the assortment of sticks to cover the wood base.

2. Glue the sticks in place with the Tacky glue.

3. Let dry overnight.

4. Choose a few of the sticks to paint with the acrylic paint. We chose a dot pattern, but you could do something different like stripes or wiggly lines. Let dry and add a hanger to the back to hang on the wall.

HINT: You can add acorns or tiny pinecones to the relief.

What you'll need:

· Liquid starch
· Piece of corrugated cardboard
· Wooden skewers
· Plastic spoons
· Jars filled with half water/half craft acrylic paint
· Plastic dishpan
· Plastic table cloth
· Cover stock white paper

MARBLEIZING

LET'S MAKE ART!

1. Fill the dishpan with liquid starch. Push the skewers through the cardboard to make a comb tool.

2. Drop different colors of the watered down paint onto the surface of the starch. Some will sink. If too much sinks, water the paint down a bit more.

3. Gently swirl the colors with the comb tool. Place your paper over the paint and lightly drop it in. Tap the four corners to contact the paint.

4. Pick it up from ONE corner and let it drip into the pan. Place on the plastic cloth to dry flat overnight. Repeat!

HINT: This paper makes beautiful cards and backgrounds for drawings!

given place, as *the streams abound in trout*; moral qualities which are inherent; as *he abounds in courage &c.*; b (followed by *with*) to be plentifully stocked with: *the British Museum abounds with old statues*.

abounding, adj. [1. abóunding; 2. abóundiŋ], fr. Pres. Part. of prec. a Being plentiful, abundant. Phr. *grace abounding*; b abounding in, *abounding with*. See prec.

about (I.), adv. [1. abóut; 2. abáut]. O.E. *abútan, onbútan*, 'around', of time, 'about'. M.E. *abúte(n)*. See a- & but, conj. 1. On all sides, around; here and there, in various directions : *to look, walk, move about*. 2. In circuit, around the outside (archaic): *a mile about*; *to come about*, to take place, happen; *to bring about*, to cause; *to take place*. 3. Nearly, approximately; closely corresponding to in quality, number, degree &c.: *about as high as, about a mile &c.* (colloq.) *just about enough, quite enough*. 4. To a reversed position, in the opposite direction : *to face about*; (mil.) *about turn !*, face the opposite direction; (naut.) *about ship !*, order to place a ship on the other tack; Phrs. *to go, set, about something*, prepare to do, start doing ; *going about* (of news, report &c.), current ; *out and about*, able to pursue one's ordinary occupation (after illness &c.); *to be about*, up and about, to be astir, not in bed ; *to put about*, see put (I.); *to send about one's business*, dismiss ; *turn and turn about*, alternately.

about (II.), prep. See prec. 1. Around, all around : *bind the chains about him* ; on every side of : *look about you* ; here and there, to and fro in : *to walk about the streets &c.* Phr. *to beat about the bush*, approach a subject indirectly, not to come straight to the point. 2. Near to, in close proximity to : by one's person : *everything handsome about him* ; *about the Court*. 3. Engaged in, concerned with (archaic) : *'I must be about My Father's business'*. a Concerning, with regard to, on the subject of : *to talk about business* ; *a book about gardening* ; b in connexion with, appertaining to : *her dress is the best thing about her*. 5. (before an infin.) On the point of, in the act of (forming Fut. Part.) : *about to shout, about to speak &c.*

above, adv., prep., & adj. [1. abáv ; 2. abáv] M.E. aboven, O.E. *abufan*, fr. a- he, 'by', q.v., & ufan, upwards , cogn. w. Germ. auf. See over. 1. adv. In a higher place, over-head, expressing (i.) motion to : *to soar above*, (ii.) rest at : *the sky above* ; b higher in power, superior in rank : *it was referred to the court above* ; c earlier in order, higher in the same page (of books &c.), earlier in same book : *as is stated above* ; d in Heaven : *there is a God above*. 2. prep. a Higher than, over (of physical relation), expressing (i.) motion to : *to fly above the clouds*, (ii.) rest at : *the balloon was floating above our heads* ; Phr. *to keep one's head above water*, to keep safe ; b superior to in any respect, beyond : *above others in ability* ; Phrs. above comprehension, above reproach, above suspicion, praise &c. ; *above meanness*, superior to ; (mod. colloq. slang) *to be above oneself*, give oneself airs, be too conceited ; c surpassing in number or quantity, more than : *above 200 members*. 3. adj. Placed, written, mentioned above or before : *the above facts, statements &c.*

above-board, adv. & adj. Above the board or table (perh. orig. card-table), in open sight, without concealment or trick, honourable : *open and above-board* (U.S.A.) **aboveboard**.

above-mentioned, adj. [1. abáv mènshúnd ; 2. abáv mênjând]. Referred to, mentioned in same book, page &c.

ab ovo, adv. [1. ab óvó ; 2. ab óuvou]. Lat. 'from the egg', see ab- & ovum. From the very beginning.

abracadabra, n. [1. ábrakadábra ; 2. æbrakadábra]. Origin unknown. A spell, magic formula, a catchword.

abrade, vb. trans. [1. abréd ; 2. abréid], fr. Lat.

---

abradere, 'to scrape off ', fr. ab- & *rādere*, 'to scrape off, shave '. See raze. To rub or wear off, wear away by friction, graze, esp. of skin.

Abraham man, n. [1. Abraham man ; 2. éibrahæm man], fr. the parable of Lazarus (Luke xvi.), (hist.) A lunatic beggar of the 16th and 17th cents., licensed to beg by Bethlehem Hospital; also one of a set of vagrant beggars pretending to be lunatics under licence.

abranchiate, adj. & n. [1. abrángkiàt ; 2. abrénkieit]. a-, 'without ', & branchiate. a adj. Not provided with gills ; b n., animal that is not provided with gills at any stage of development.

abrasion, n. [1. abrázhun ; 2. abréiзan], fr. Lat. *abrāsion-(em)*, fr. *abrās-(um)*, P.P. type of abrādere. See abrade. 1. a Grazing, rubbing, or scraping off, as of the skin ; b place where skin is scraped off. 2. a A wearing down, rubbing away, as of rocks, machinery &c. ; b place showing this.

abrasive, adj. & n. [1. abráziv ; 2. abréiziv]. Prec. w. Lat. suff. *-īvus*. See -ive. 1. adj. a Tending to graze, scrape the skin ; b tending to wear down, rub away rocks &c. 2. n. Substance, such as emery &c., used for grinding, polishing &c.

abraxas, n. [1. abráksas ; 2. abréksas]. Formed of the Gk. letters as numerals, equiv. to 365. 1. a A mystic name, used by the Egyptian Gnostics of the Supreme Being as ruling 365 heavens ; b a gem engraved with this name, used as a talisman. 2. (entom.) A genus of buff-coloured moths spotted with black, the magpie moth.

abreast, adv. [1. abrést ; 2. abrést]. a- & breast. a a In a level with, when facing or moving in same direction ; b (fig.) *abreast of*, or, more rarely, with, keeping up with, not behind the advance of science, thought &c. ; *abreast of the times, of what is going on &c.*

abridge, vb. trans. [1. abríj ; 2. abridʒ]. M.E. abregge, fr. O. Fr. abreger, 'shorten', Mod. Fr. abreger, fr. Lat. abbreviare, 'to shorten '. See abbreviate. To make shorter, lessen, diminish, curtail ; esp. to shorten by using fewer words, to condense (books &c.).

abridg(e)ment, n. [1. abríjment ; 2. abrídʒment]. Prec. & -ment. Shortening, reduction, diminution, condensation ; curtailment (of rights) ; specif., reduced or condensed form of a book.

abroad, adv. [1. abráwd ; 2. abró:d]. M.E. abrood. See a- & broad. 1. a Broadly, widely, at large, over a wide space ; *publish, spread abroad* (of rumour, news &c.) ; b current, going about (of rumours &c.) : *there is a rumour abroad*. 2. Outside one's abode, out of doors : *to be abroad early*. 3. Beyond the bounds of a country ; in foreign lands : *to go, travel, abroad* ; (colloq., fig.) *to be all abroad*, to be puzzled, confused in mind. Treated as a noun in Phr. *from abroad &c.*

abrogate, vb. trans. [1. ábrogāt ; 2. ǽbrogeit], fr. Lat. *abrogāt-(um)*, P.P. type of abrogāre, 'to repeal ' (law &c.), fr. ab- & rogāre, 'to ask, propose ' (as a law). See rogation. To repeal, annul, abolish (laws or customs).

abrogation, n. [1. abrogāshun ; 2. æbrageiʃən]. Prec. & -ion. Act of repealing by authority.

abrupt, adj. [1. abrúpt ; 2. abrápt], fr. Lat. *abrupt-(um)*, P.P. type of abrumpere, 'to break off '. See ab- & rupture. 1. Broken off, steep, craggy (of rocks, banks, precipices &c.). 2. Sudden, hasty, unexpected ; a abrupt entrance, departure (of actions) ; b short, uncivil, gruff. 3 (of manners) short, uncivil, gruff. 4 (style) Breaking off suddenly, disconnected, passing from one thought to another without proper transition. 4. (geol., of strata) Suddenly cropping out.

abruptly, adv. Prec. & -ly. In an abrupt manner ; suddenly, without warning.

abruptness, n. See prec. & -ness. Quality of being abrupt ; suddenness, unceremon-

---

haste in speech, manners &c.

abscess, n. [1. abscs, -sis ; 2. ǽbses, -sis]. Lat. abscessus, 'going away ', fr. abscédere, 'go away ', fr. abs- (for ab-) & cédere, see cede ; sense being 'flowing of humours into one channel '. Inflamed swelling on the body containing pus ; sac or cavity filled with pus in an organ of the body.

abscind, vb. trans. [1. absínd ; 2. absínd], fr. Lat. abscindere, 'to cut off ', fr. ab- & scindere, 'to cut, split ', Pret. scidi, P.P. scissum (fr. *scid-tom), cogn. w. Gk. skhizô, 'split', skhisma, 'cleft, division '. See schism. From variant of same base, Aryan *skhid-, we get Goth. skaidan, 'divide ', O.E. *scēadan, 'divide, distinguish '. See shed (I.). To cut off (obs.).

Abscissa

abscissa, n. [1. absísa ; 2. absísa]. Lat. abscissa (linea), see prec. word. A line cut off, as point of reference in geometry.

abscission, n. [1. absíshun ; 2. absíʃan], fr. Lat. abscissio-(um), P.P. type of abscindere, see abscind, & -ion. Cutting off ; state of separation.

abscond, vb. intrans. [1. abskónd ; 2. abskónd], fr. Lat. abscondere, 'to put out of sight, conceal ', fr. abs- (for ab-) & condere. The history of this vb. is remarkable. It comes fr. Lat. cum, 'together ', & base *dhē-, 'make, put ', cogn. w. Lat. facio, 'make ', Pret. fē-ci. Orig. sense is 'put together, build ', then 'put away together, store up ', then 'to hide '. For other words fr. base *dhē- see do, deed, thesis, fact. To depart secretly and suddenly ; steal off and hide oneself ; esp. to run away to escape the law.

absconder, n. [1. abskónder ; 2. abskónda]. Prec. & -er. One who absconds.

absence, n. [1. ábsens ; 2. ǽbsans]. Fr., fr. Lat. absentia, fr. absens, Pres. Part. of abesse, 'to be absent ', fr. ab- & esse, 'to be '. See essence. 1. The state of being away from a place or from company ; opposed to presence. 2. The time of being away : *long absence &c.* 3. Non-existence, lack, want of : absence of evidence &c. 4. Mental abstraction, inattention, esp. in Phr. absence of mind. 5. (at Eton College) Roll-call.

absent (I.), adj. [1. ábsent ; 2. ǽbsant], fr. Lat. absens, absentia, Pres. Part. of abesse. See absence. 1. Not present, being away in another place : absent friends. 2 Mentally abstracted, inattentive to what is going on around one, preoccupied, having the mind withdrawn from what is passing ; absent-minded : an absent air.

absent (II.), vb. trans. [1. absént ; 2. absént], fr. Fr. absenter, fr. Lat. absentāre. See prec. (used reflex.) To remain away, withdraw (oneself) intentionally : to absent oneself from a meeting &c.

absentee, n. [1. ábsentē ; 2. æbsantí], fr. absent & -ee. A person not present, esp. one who absents himself on an occasion when he ought to be present ; one habitually living away from home ; specif., a landlord not living on his estate.

absenteeism, n. [1. ábsentēīzm ; 2. æbsanti-

COFFEE PAINTINGS

LET'S MAKE ART!

1. Using the soft brush dip into the coffee. You will use it just like you would watercolor paints.

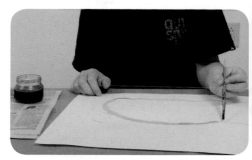

2. Paint a picture with the coffee on the white paper.

3. To make darker areas go over the same places twice, let the first part dry before going over it.

4. Try to make a painting on an old book page. The aged color of the book page works nicely with the coffee color paint.

HINT: If you want to add color let the coffee dry and add crayon in between.

What you'll need:

· Two old book pages
· Clear glue
· Wooden bead
· Needle and thread

LET'S MAKE ART!

1. Fold one book page across the short side back and forth like a paper fan. Fold the other book page along the long side the same way.

2. Fold the long page in half and glue it together to make the skirt.

3. Thread the needle with 12 inches (30cm) of thread. Push the needle through the center of the folded skirt and through the center of the folded wings.

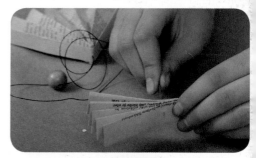

4. Sew the bead on through the hole and tie a knot to secure the bead to the wings. Cut off the needle and knot the thread to create the hanger. Make 50 of these to hang on a big tree branch! Add a string of lights!

What you'll need:

· Pinecone and twigs

· Soft brush

· Paper plate

· Craft acrylic paints

· Wax paper

· Embroidery floss or thin string

LET'S MAKE ART!

1. Paint a long stick with as many colors as you like. Leave some of the stick unpainted. Paint some short twigs different colors, leaving half unpainted. Let dry on wax paper.

2. Tie the string on one end of the long stick. To form a hanger, cut the string to desired length and tie to the remaining end.

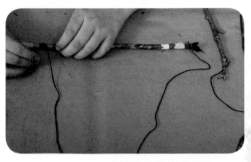

3. Tie the pinecone onto the stick as shown using two lengths of string – one on each end of the pinecone.

4. Hang your mobile on the wall to finish it. Cut a string for every two twigs, making them all the same length. Tie a twig to each end of the string. Hang the string with the twigs over the pinecone. Adjust the twigs to hang the way you choose. Hang it outside or inside to enjoy a little nature!

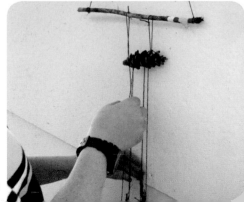

What you'll need:
- Black paper and white paper
- White craft paint
- Paper plate
- Twig
- Cotton swab
- String
- Cardboard rectangle
- Scissors
- Masking tape
- Clear glue
- Newspaper to protect work area

LET'S MAKE ART!

1. Wrap the string around the cardboard and tape it to the back to hold it. Put some white paint onto the paper plate. Dip the string into the paint and first print it on the newspaper then onto the black paper. Fill up the black paper with the print.

Hint: Less paint makes better prints!

2. Dip the cotton swab in the paint and print onto the paper to create small snow-like flakes.

3. Break the twig into sections and glue down to make a tree.

4. Draw an owl or other night creatures on the white paper. Cut it out and glue to the black paper to complete your mixed media painting.

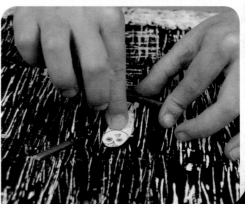

What you'll need:

· Paper Tubes
· Scissors
· Acrylic craft paint
· Paper plates
· Paper
· Newspaper to protect the workspace

LET'S MAKE ART!

1. Cut slits around one end of the tube as shown. Bend them back to make petal shapes.

2. Pour the paint onto the paper plate. Dip the uncut edge into one color and print the flower centers on the paper. Press hard enough to get a good print.

3. Print the petals by dipping into the same or different color paint over the flower center circles.

4. Using the side of the tube or different sized tube, dip into the paint and print the stems of the flowers.

HINT: You may cut the end of the petals into shapes to make different flowers.

What you'll need:

· Large paper
· Pencil
· Watercolor set
· Soft brush
· Water
· A friend can help too!

LET'S MAKE ART!

1. Draw around your arm and hand on the paper. Have a friend draw around yours and you can draw around theirs! Draw three or four or more overlapping arms and hands.

2. Inside the hands and arms, draw other shapes to create patterns or new lines.

3. Paint the new shapes you have drawn, using as many colors as you choose.

4. Paint the background too! Remember to let the paint dry before painting an area right next to the wet paint – or it will run. Paint in different sections to avoid this. Or let it run and experiment with new colors.

What you'll need:

· Flat round rocks
· Thick glue
· Air-dry clay (found on page 142)
· Moss
· White and yellow craft paint
· Finepoint marker
· Moss, driftwood and pinecone

LET'S MAKE ART!

1. With the white paint make eyes on the rocks. With the yellow paint make a beak. Let dry completely.

2. Use the finepoint marker to create details in the eyes and around the beak. Create wings and draw feathers around the back of the owl, too!

3. Use a little air-dry clay on the bottom of the rocks to hold them in place on the driftwood. Add glue to the bottom of the clay and press firmly onto the wood.

4. Add the moss and pinecone with glue to cover the clay. Add any other bits of nature you find!

LET'S MAKE ART!

1. Arrange the paper rings onto the cardboard backing. You can make anything with these rings!

2. Glue the rings onto the cardboard, let dry overnight or several hours,

3. Tear small pieces of tissue paper to cover the background. Put some glue on the background, then stick the tissue to the background. Secure them by brushing over them with the water-thinned glue.

4. Finish the rings with tissue paper and paint.

What you'll need:

· Sliding style matchbox
· Acrylic craft paint
· Tiny detail brush
· Water
· Pencil and Markers
· Tiny twig and glue
· White ink pen
· Fine point pen

LET'S MAKE ART!

1. Paint the matchbox white and let dry. Draw a tree inside and add an animal in the tree. Draw the rest of the tree on the outside of the box.

2. Paint the tree and animals with a tiny brush. Let dry.

3. When the paint is completely dry add details with the fine point pen, white ink pen and markers as you choose.

4. Glue the twig into the tree on the inside. Think up new scenes for your next matchbox! How about a beach scene with a tiny shell or a garden with a tiny butterfly?

What you'll need:

· Acrylic craft paints
· Water
· Newspaper
· Soft brush
· UHU glue stick
· Scissors
· Corrugated cardboard

LET'S MAKE ART!

1. Paint a sky and background on a piece of cardboard. Let dry.

2. From the columns of the newspaper cut tall buildings. Use different sections of the newspaper. Small print without photos works well. Make each of the tops of the buildings different shapes.

3. Arrange them on the background to create a city. Overlap the buildings to create a crowded scene. Glue them down and press hard to make them stick.

4. Use some watered down craft paint to add a little color to the buildings if desired.

What you'll need:

· Drinking straw
· Watercolor paints
· Acrylic craft paints
· Paper tube
· Heavyweight paper
· Water
· Soft brush
· Paper plate

LET'S MAKE ART!

1. Wet the soft brush with water and a lot of watercolor paint to make a few drops at the bottom of your paper. Blow toward the drops using the straw in short bursts to create the tree trunk. Continue blowing in short bursts close to the droplets until you have the size trunk you want.

2. Flatten the cardboard tube into an oval-leaf shape. Put some acrylic paint in different colors (you choose! You are the artist!) on the paper plate. Dip the tube into the paint and print a leaf onto the tree.

3. Continue dipping the paint and printing leaves with the tube. Dip into the paint each time for a good print.

4. Change colors and fill your paper with leaves.

What you'll need:

· Colorful paper (or paint your
  own with watercolor)
· Pencil
· String or embroidery floss
· Thick glue
· Beads
· Hole punch

LET'S MAKE ART!

1. Cut the paper into four 9 inch by 6 inch (22 x 15cm) rectangles. Fold them in an accordion or fan like fold along the long edge, using a pencil to crease them.

2. Fold in half and attach with a thick glue to hold it together. This makes one quarter of the circle. Make three more.

3. Glue the four accordion folded quarters together to create a circle. Punch a hole at the top.

4. Tie a string or embroidery floss through the hole to make a hanger. Add beads if desired. Make a few and hang them up in your room!

BLACK GLUE PAINTING

LET'S MAKE ART!

1. Choose what you want to draw. We chose flowers. With a pencil, draw the outline of your subject on your paper.

2. Mix 2 oz of black craft acrylic paint with a half a bottle of clear glue. Dispense the black glue over the lines you drew in pencil. Let dry overnight.

3. When dry, use the watercolors to paint in the colors as you choose.

4. Don't use too much water and your colors will be brighter!

What you'll need:

- Small balls of yarn in assorted colors
- Two thin sticks, chopsticks or thin dowels
- Thick glue

OJO DE DIOS

LET'S MAKE ART!

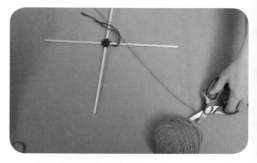

1. Place your dowels in the shape of a cross. Glue them together where they cross and let dry.

2. Tie the first color of yarn to one of the sticks at the center of the cross. Wrap it around that stick twice, then wrap it around the next stick once, then the third stick once and then the fourth stick (back where you started) once.

3. Keep wrapping around once all the way around your sticks until you want to change colors. Cut the yarn and tie on a new color of yarn and continue wrapping around your sticks.

4. Change color as often as you like. Wrap until it almost covers the sticks. Tie a knot at the last stick wrapped so it doesn't unravel. Make a loop to hang it!

HINT: You can make tiny Ojo de Dios with toothpicks and embroidery floss!

What you'll need:

· Scrap wood
· Old book or music pages
· Clear glue
· Wide brush for glue
· Acrylic craft paint
· Charcoal or crayon
· Water
· Paper plate palette
· Paintbrush for details

OLD PAPER PAINTING

LET'S MAKE ART!

1. Tear the pages into small sections. Apply the glue with a brush onto the wood. Stick the pages to the wood and brush glue over the top to cover the paper.

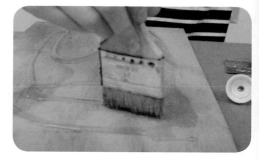

2. Fill the board completely with paper and overlap where you choose. Let dry.

3. Draw a bouquet of flowers either from a photo or a garden or even make one up! Use the charcoal or crayon for a beautiful, bold outline.

4. Paint the flowers, centers and leaves inside of what you drew to make the drawing come alive. Hang on the wall for everyone to see!

What you'll need:

· Air Dry Clay (recipe on page 142)
· Wooden skewer
· Waxed linen cord or thin string
· Assorted colors of acrylic paints
· Soft brush and water
· Newspaper to cover area
· Waxed paper to dry beads

COLORFUL BEADS

LET'S MAKE ART!

1. Squeeze the clay to make it smooth. Pinch off a small pea-sized amount of clay. Roll into a ball. Push the skewer through the clay to form a hole. Let dry for two days or until hard.

2. When dry and completely hard, paint each of the beads an assortment of colors. Dry on the waxed paper to keep from sticking.

3. Put the cord around your neck to measure how long it should be. Cut to length. Thread the beads onto the cord.

4. Make a pattern with the different colors. Tie a knot at the end and wear you new jewelry!

HINT: Try making different shaped beads: tubes, triangles and squares!

What you'll need:

· Small items from a junk drawer
· Tacky glue
· Cardboard base for the sculpture

LET'S MAKE ART!

1. Look around the house or yard for small items that interest you. Recycled items are always great!

2. Try putting different pieces of junk together to create a person or thing. Balance is important – smaller things on top with larger things on the bottom work best.

3. Start gluing from the bottom up. Let the layers dry in between gluing for a stronger base.

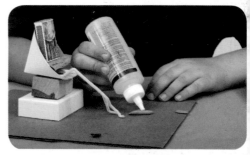

4. Add small details last. Display your sculpture on a shelf where everyone can see it! Give your sculpture a name!

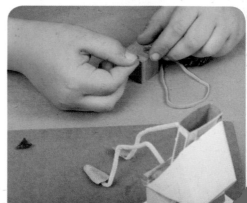

What you'll need:

· Recycled file folder
· Acrylic craft paints
· Soft brush
· Paper plate
· Water
· Scissors
· Pencil and ruler

LET'S MAKE ART!

1. With a pencil and ruler draw the largest triangle possible on the file folder. Cut out and trace a second one on the remaining folder. Cut out the second one.

2. Paint each triangle on both sides with the acrylic craft paint. Try using lots of colors or just a few. It's up to you as you are the artist! Let dry.

3. Cut a slit from the top to the middle of one triangle. Cut a slit from the bottom up to the middle from the other triangle.

4. Put the two triangles together joining them at the slits. Stand it up to display. You could make an entire forest!

HINT: Make trees of all sizes by changing the size of the triangles. Add glitter for snowy trees!

What you'll need:

· Paste paper recipe (page 142)
· Sheets of large paper
· Plastic table cloth to work on
· Combs, paper tubes and
  plastic gift cards
· Spray bottle with water
· Foam brush

LET'S MAKE ART!

1. Spray a large sheet of paper with water until completely wet. With the sponge brush paint a thick layer of paste paint to the paper.

2. Use the comb to create lines.

3. Twist the gift card on the paper to make bow shapes.

4. Use the paper tubes to make circles! Let it dry on the plastic table cloth so it doesn't stick.

HINT: You can iron the paper flat when it is dry.

What you'll need:

· Paste papers you made on page 87
· White papers slightly smaller than your paste paper
· UHU glue stick
· Large nail
· Hammer
· Piece of wood
· Embroidery floss
· Pencil

LET'S MAKE ART!

1. Fold the paste paper in half and crease the fold with the side of a pencil. This is now the cover. Fold the white paper the same way. Place the white papers inside the paste paper cover. Open to the middle of the book and place it on the wooden board.

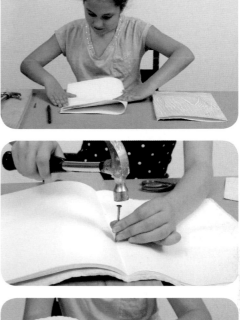

2. With the hammer pound the nail through the folds a quarter way down from the top edge and a quarter way up from the bottom to create a two holes all the way through the pages and cover.

3. From the inside center page, thread each of the ends of the floss through one of the holes. It might be easier threading through the pages first and then through the cover. Using the nail or a needle can be helpful. Gently pull tight!

4. Tie at the outside of the cover with a knot to secure. Add collaged letters or designs to the front cover if you want to! Make a drawing every day in it!

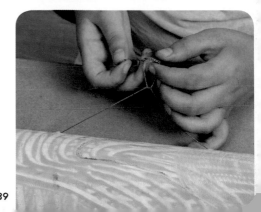

What you'll need:

- Yarn – multicolored variegated is nice!
- Thin string or waxed linen cord
- Paper or foam plate
- Scissors
- Masking tape

LET'S MAKE ART!

1. Cut slits around the plate about one inch (2.5 cm) apart. Tape the string to the back of the plate. Wrap the string through one slit to the front and then across to the slit opposite it and around to the back. Continue wrapping moving to the next slit until you are at the back and all the slits are filled. Cut the string and tape to secure.

2. Begin weaving by starting in the very center. Cut a long piece of yarn and put it under one of the center strings and pull until it is almost at the end of the length of yarn. Press a finger or two onto the center of the string and yarn end with one hand and weave the other end over and under pulling the yarn through the strings.

3. Keep going over and under around the strings with the yarn.

4. Tie on new yarn to weave all the way to the outside of the plate. Tie the end and hide the knot in back of the weaving.

What you'll need:
· Modeling clay
· Hot glue (use with an adult!)
· Tiny jar with a tight-fitting lid
· Paint or marker
· Glitter

LET'S MAKE ART!

1. Using the clay model a creature as the focus of your snow globe. We made a Yeti. Add details with paint or markers.

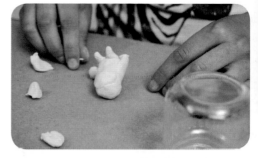

2. With an adult, hot glue the creature to the inside of the jar lid.

3. Fill the jar with water. Add a generous amount of glitter.

4. Screw the lid on tightly! Shake it up and watch it snow inside.

What you'll need:

· Air dry clay (recipe on page 142)
· Craft acrylic paints
· Soft paintbrush
· Toothpicks
· Thick glue

LET'S MAKE ART!

1. Knead enough clay to create a small ball that will fit in your hand. Knead until smooth. Create a base for your landscape. Make it thick enough to stick a toothpick into it one third of the toothpick's length.

2. Model trees and birds or animals. Keep them tiny to fit on your landscape.

3. Stick the toothpick into the bottom of the objects and stand them up in the clay base. Add a drop of thick glue to the hole if it seems wobbly.

4. Let dry for three days or until hard. This time varies with weather conditions. Paint as desired with the craft acrylic paints.

HINT: This clay is easy to make with an adult!

What you'll need:
· Dark construction paper
· Waxed paper
· UHU glue stick
· Pencil
· Scissors
· Colorful tissue paper

LET'S MAKE ART!

1. Draw around a plate with a pencil to make a circle on the dark construction paper. Cut out the circle by folding the paper as shown.

2. Cut a piece of waxed paper a little larger than the circle.

3. Cut or tear colorful tissue paper into shapes. Use a glue stick to glue the tissue to the waxed paper. Make your own pattern. Anything goes!

4. Tissue paper side up, position the circle over the top of the waxed paper and glue together. Hang in a sunny window and let the sun shine through!

What you'll need:

- Cardboard rectangle
- Plastic needle
- Yarn (one color for the loom and many colors for weaving)
- Fork
- Pencil and ruler
- Scissors
- Masking tape

TINY LOOM

LET'S MAKE ART!

1. Mark the cardboard with pencil lines every ¼ inch (6mm) across the long way. Cut slits on the pencil marks and wind the yarn tightly around the cardboard into the slits as shown. Tape the end to the backside of the loom.

2. Thread the needle with the first color of yarn, start to weave by going under the first yarn on the loom, over the second, under the third and over the next. Under—over—under—over all the way to the end.

3. Turn and go back starting with "over" if the last stitch was "under" or "under" if your last stitch was "over". Change colors of yarn. Unthread the needle and trim the end long enough for a fringe. Keep weaving until the tiny loom is full.

4. Use the fork to move the weaving more tightly together. This makes a great little wall hanging for a doll house or a pretty piece of art to give to someone special.

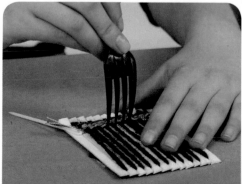

TISSUE PAPER PORTRAIT

LET'S MAKE ART!

1. Draw your face (made up or real!) on the heavyweight paper.

2. Start tearing the tissue paper into smaller pieces for the hair, skin and shoulders.

3. Use the scissors for smaller details if desired – eyes, nose mouth.

4. Mix a little water into the glue to make it thinner and easier to spread. Brush the background paper with the glue where you want to place the tissue paper. Work in small sections. Stick the tissue paper down into the glue and brush over the tissue to seal. Take your time and go slowly!

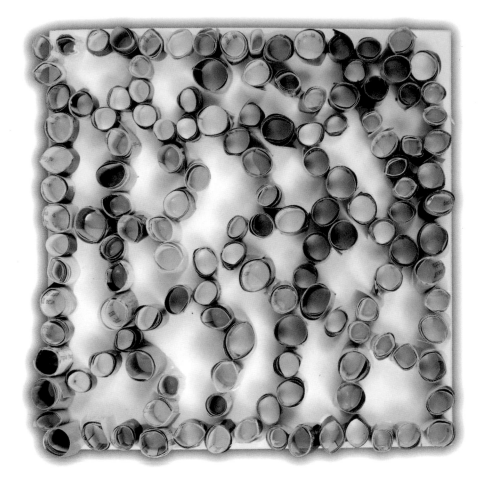

What you'll need:
· Colorful magazine pages
· UHU glue stick
· Clear glue
· Cardboard or matte board
  for backing

LET'S MAKE ART!

1. Cut magazine pages into thin strips. Vary the widths of the strips, all under an inch (2.5cm).

2. Apply the UHU glue to one side of the magazine strip. Loosely roll it up. Secure the end with a little more glue.

3. Put a drop of clear glue on the backing board. Place the roll on end and press it firmly.

4. Keep adding the rolls of paper to the board to create a design all your own!

HINT: build this project over a few days as it takes time to build a whole relief!

What you'll need:

· Small wooden hoop
· Thin string
· Air Dry Clay (recipe on page 142)
· Assorted acrylic craft paints
· Wooden Skewer
· Round cookie cutter or glass
· Rolling pin

LET'S MAKE ART!

1. Squeeze clay until smooth. Roll out clay. Cut out circles. Allow to dry, turning them over if necessary.

2. Paint the circles on both sides with a bulls-eye pattern using the colors you choose. Let dry.

3. Cut the string into different lengths to hang the bulls-eye circles from the hoop. Tie them around the hoop.

4. Cut three strings the same length to make a hanger. Tie it onto the hoop to form a triangle so it will hang straight.

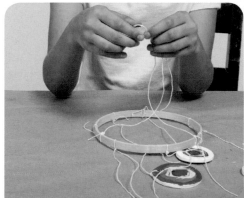

HINT: You can paint flowers or animals or cut out different shapes for a different mobile.

What you'll need:

· Felt
· Embroidery floss
· Tacky glue
· Embroidery needle
· Scissors
· Paper and pencil
· Black permanent marker

LET'S MAKE ART!

1. Choose a creature to create. With a pencil draw a rectangle that is three times wider than your finger onto the paper. This will be your pattern. Round out one end of the rectangle for the head and add ears. Create a face with a circle or oval. If you want arms you can draw those as a separate pattern too! Cut out the pattern pieces.

2. Place your pattern on the felt and draw around it with the marker. Cut out the pieces following the lines you drew.

3. Glue on the face. From the felt cut out small details such as eyes or a nose. Glue them on, too! Add a tummy and arms if you want to! Let dry overnight.

4. Thread the needle with the embroidery floss and tie a knot at the end. Stitch the front to the back starting at the bottom of the rectangle and work your way along the edge. Leave the bottom open for your finger.

What you'll need:

- · Black marker
- · Gel pen
- · Pencil
- · Copy paper
- · Scissors
- · UHU Glue stick
- · Marbleized paper (page 49)
- · Large colorful background paper

LET'S MAKE ART!

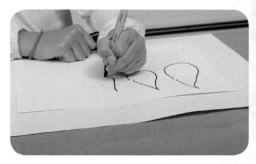

1. With the marker make three sizes of raindrop shapes (small, medium, large) on the copy paper. These will be patterns for your feathers.

2. Cut out the shapes and trace them onto your marbleized papers (that you made on page 49). Then cut out the shapes from the marbleized paper. Make enough to fill your background paper!

3. Arrange them on the background paper. Draw a body for the peacock with a pencil on another marbleized paper. It can look like an bowling pin shape or a thin oval. Cut it out and glue it down to the background paper.

4. Add the feathers around the peacock. Glue them down. Add eyes and a beak and some peacock feet with the marker or gel pens.

HINT: Make a small peacock on a folded piece of paper for a special greeting card.

HINT: Hang this in a room where there is a breeze so it will spin!

What you'll need:

· Coffee stir sticks
· Pencil
· Clear glue
· Thin string or waxed linen cord
· Tissue paper in assorted colors
· Scissors
· Straight pin
· Embroidery hoop

LET'S MAKE ART!

1. Glue three sticks together to create a triangle. Let dry for several hours.

2. Trace around the triangle with a pencil on the tissue paper. Cut out the triangle.

3. Spread clear glue on the stick triangle and place the tissue paper triangle onto the glue. Make eight triangles in different colors.

4. Poke a small hole in the corner of one side of the paper with a pin to tie a string to hang them from the hoop. Tie the triangles on the hoop at two different lengths of string for a two layer effect. Cut three lengths of string the same length to make a hanger for the mobile.

What you'll need:

· Styrofoam ball
· Small jar
· Clear glue
· Toothpicks
· UHU glue
· Discarded magazine pages

LET'S MAKE ART!

1. Cut strips from magazine pages in varying widths – no wider than the toothpicks. Apply UHU glue to the length of the magazine strip and roll up tightly.

2. Stick three toothpicks in the Styrofoam ball to secure it to the jar. Stick another into the ball and slip a magazine roll over it and glue it with the clear glue to the ball.

3. Keep adding more toothpicks and rolls adding glue between the rolls and under each roll. Let dry completely when finished. This is a multi-day project that is easy but takes a lot of time.

4. When you are finished tie a piece of string or clear fishing line to a toothpick on either side of Sputnik and hang it from the ceiling. It's your very own satellite!

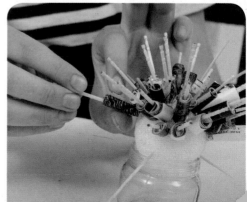

HINT: Find out about the real Sputnik at your local library!

Inspiration comes from many places for artists.

Nature is filled with so much inspiration – from a tiny seed to an ocean and everything in between.

Sometimes a city that has busy streets and tall buildings can inspire an artist to draw or sculpt.

Music can inspire visual art and dance can inspire poetry!

Artists inspire each other and often they can work together making art.

Visiting a gallery or art museum can spark an idea and inspire you to create something new.

This section, the artist gallery, is filled with some artists who inspire me. They work with interesting materials and make beautiful art.

What inspires you?

LISA SOLOMON

MIXED MEDIA ARTIST

Lisa Solomon is a mixed media artist
that moonlights as an art professor,
illustrator, craft book author and
graphic designer.

Lisa loved rainbows as a kid and is still completely and totally in love with arranging things in color order. She has shown her work in galleries all over the United States and even all over the world [gasp!].

Her work is research-based and takes her in all different directions. She's learned a lot about the importance of the number 1000 in Japanese culture [she's a happa], migration, chemical toxins, traditional pigments and where they come from, fugo balloon bombs and WWII tanks, and color theory amongst many other things.

Lisa also loves instant photography, onigiri [rice balls], mochi of all kinds, and bobba tea. She lives and works in Oakland, California with her husband, young daughter, a pit bull, a long-haired dachshund mutt, two three-legged kitties, a tank of fish, and many many many spools of thread.

www.lisasolomon.com

ED EMBERLEY

AUTHOR AND ILLUSTRATOR

Ed Emberley is a much beloved, award winning author and illustrator of books for children. He created his "drawing alphabet" in the 1970's. Using simple shapes, dots and lines, he shows you how to draw just about anything in the world! He applied this alphabet to thumbprints with The Great Thumbprint Drawing Book.

www.edemberley.com

Planes, trains and automobiles

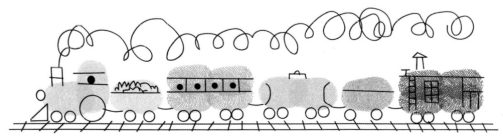

MIMI KIRCHNER

FABRIC ARTIST

I have been an artist and a maker my whole life. Doing projects and playing with all kinds of materials were what my childhood was made of. By High School, I was making jewelry and selling it. I went to art school and studied drawing, metals, fiber arts and clay with some business classes too. I knew I wanted to make my living with my art.

After graduating from College, I spent 20 years making decorated functional pottery tableware and selling it through craft galleries. In 1999, I admitted to myself that I was no longer excited or inspired by the pottery and went on a search for a new way to express myself. While I was trying out some new art forms- painting, printmaking- I was re- discovering sewing, knitting, crochet and other fiber-related arts.

I got interested in folk art portraits and discovered that people had painted cloth dolls in the same folk art style. I was so inspired to try to make something similar and soon, that was all I wanted to do! Doll-making had taken over my life.

www.mimikirchner.com

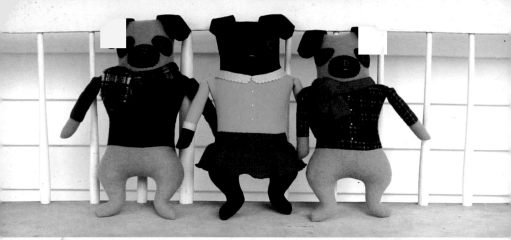

These days, I make a variety of dolls, mixing fabrics from old clothing and new fabrics. I hand-dye some of the fabrics so that they are one-of-a-kind. I love combining colors, embroidering the faces,

MOLLY GRANT
CORDWAINER (SHOEMAKER)

Molly Grant began leatherworking in her early 20's, first by working on her own and then by apprenticing at the Black Swan Leather shop in Portsmouth, NH, where she learned the basic skills of traditional leatherworking.

Molly first saw Cordwainer Shoes when she was ten years old at the League of New Hampshire Craftsmen's Fair, known nationally as the oldest craft fair in the nation. She became a juried member in 1989, and participated by showing her line of handbags. There, she had the opportunity to meet Paul Mathews, owner of the Cordwainer Shop. Within a few months' time Molly was traveling to craft shows nationally with Paul and learning the Cordwainer art.

Molly still makes handbags, but the main business is footwear and teaching shoemaking workshops at the shop and at craft schools across the country.

www.cordwainershop.com

JUDITH HELLER CASSELL

PRINTMAKER AND SCULPTOR

I was born in a log cabin in the foothills of Virginia and those days spent living and playing in the shadow of the Blue Ridge Mountains are the spirit behind most of my work. In my etchings, woodcuts, collagraphs, and sculpture, I attempt to capture those long ago feelings.

Drawing in the dirt was one of my earliest memories. I still remember the warmth of the sun on my back, the feel of the soil beneath my fingers, and the thrill of the magic that formed those pictures in the soft earth beneath our swings. Our dirt was a wonderful color red that sometimes I would mix with water and use as paint. I still have buckets of this fantastic colored earth that I continue to use.

Nothing gives me greater pleasure than for someone to like my work, but first I must like it. As an artist, I change what I actually see into what I feel about what I see.

When a picture or sculpture appears that pleases me, it is a joy beyond measure – and THAT is what makes me do what I do!

ADAM PEARSON

METAL SCULPTOR

I am a sculptor and craftsman and work as the Art Department Technician at a university.

As a kid I had much fun building things, using tools, scrounging for materials, and just making stuff. When I was old enough, I went to work for my father doing construction. I have always enjoyed landscaping and moving rocks and dirt around. For me, sculpture gives the opportunity to explore the best parts about these different experiences I had growing up and lets me use any of the possible mediums I am drawn to.

Balancing rocks and working with found materials was a way for me to combine landscape design and construction so I could present the end product as sculpture, finding beauty in the decayed and discarded.

My favorite materials to work with is steel, or really just about any metal, both found or fabricated, but I also enjoy using clay, wood, and stone.

www.pearsonsculpture.com

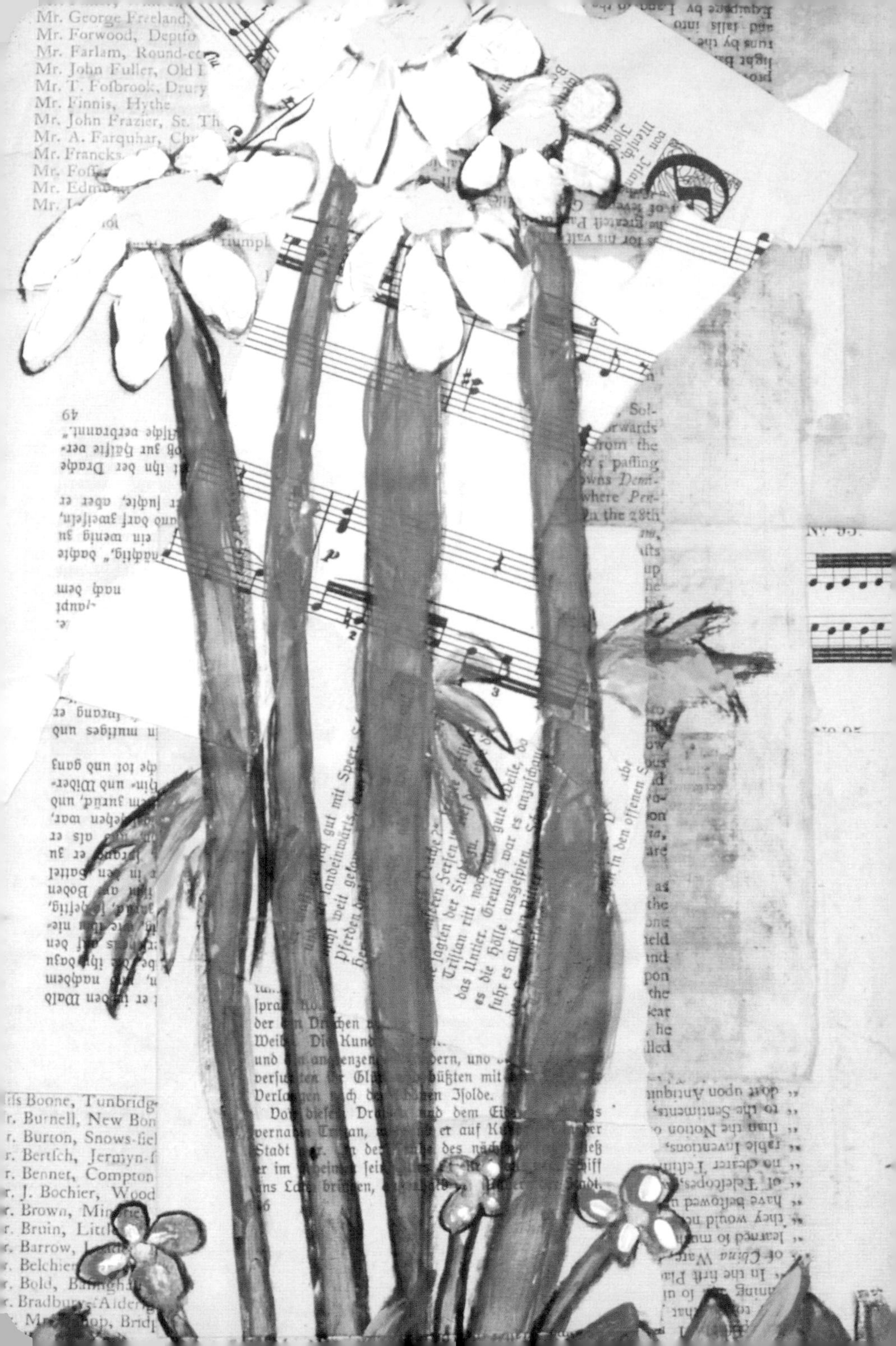

THE ART CAMP KIDS

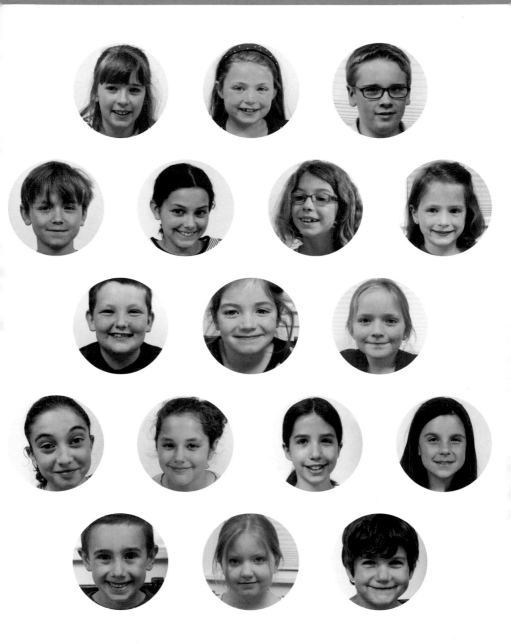

Thank you for your beautiful artwork: Addison, Alaina, Arianna, Ethan, Graham, Greta, Harper, Isabel, Jillian, Kathrine, Lillian, Liz, Lucie, Miles, Ruby, Sivi, Tom

RECIPES

Paste Papers
¼ cup cornstarch
1¾ cups water

Mix the cornstarch with ¼ cup of cold water. With a whisk, add one
cup of water and cook over a medium high heat until it is as thick as
pudding. Take of stove and add the remaining water. This will thin it
out, but as it cools, it will thicken up again. Cool in the refrigerator
for an hour. Place five tablespoons into a small jar and add one
tablespoons of acrylic craft paint. Store in a cool place.

Amazing Air Dry Clay
2 cups baking soda
1½ cups cornstarch
1½ cups water

Mix all the ingredients in a pot with a whisk over medium heat. Stir
the mixture with the whisk constantly. When it begins to form a stiff
mixture, beat well and take off the heat. Transfer into a bowl and
cover with a wet dishcloth. When cool knead into a ball and store in
an air tight plastic bag. The clay objects can be painted after they are
air dried!

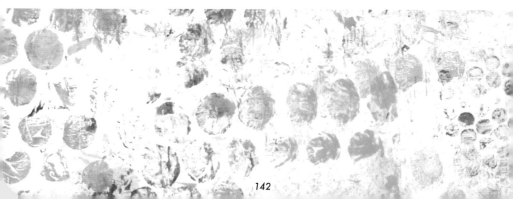

RESOURCES

Australia
Eckersley's Arts, Crafts,
and Imagination
www.eckersleys.com.au

Canada
Curry's Art Store
www.currys.com

DeSerres
www.deserres.ca

Michaels
www.michaels.com

Opus Framing & Art Supplies
www.opusframing.com

France
Graphigro
www.graphigro-paris11.fr

Italy
Vertecchi
www.vertecchi.com

United Kingdom
T N Lawrence & Son Ltd.
www.lawrence.co.uk

Creative Crafts
www.creativecrafts.co.uk

United States
A. C. Moore
www.acmoore.com

Daniel Smith
www.danielsmith.com

Dick Blick
www.dickblick.com

Jo-Ann Fabric and Craft Stores
www.joann.com

Michaels
www.michaels.com

Utrecht
www.utrechtart.com

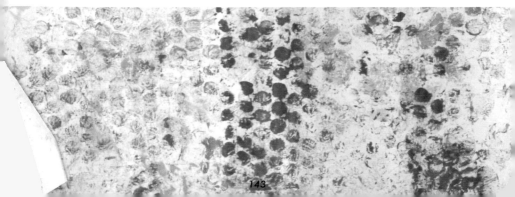

ABOUT THE AUTHOR

Susan Schwake is an artist, art educator, and author.

Her passion for teaching art has found her working in diverse settings for over 20 years. She has inspired thousands of people in private and public schools, community organizations, special needs agencies, teachers, summer camps, intergenerational facilities, libraries, and her own art school, artstream in Dover, New Hampshire.

Susan's fourth book – first in the Kid's Art series – Art for All Seasons features all new seasonally inspired creative art projects. This series follows the release of her first three books from the bestselling Art Lab for Kids series, which have been translated into five languages. The new series features her husband Rainer's layout and design, including hundreds of photographs that the couple styled and photographed together. Besides the books they work together at artstream promoting and creating graphic, web and media design work.

As a mixed media painter she feels less limited in her materials choices. Making art is a daily practice for her and she exhibits her work in galleries around the country and sometimes far away places! Susan has also created large-scale, site-specific outdoor works for public display. She is inspired by the beauty as well as decay of the natural world and people she has yet to meet. Working with children has helped her allow play and experimentation to be an important part of her own art practice!

Susan has taken her classroom online with a series of e-courses at www.susanschwake.com/class

www.susanschwake.com
www.susanschwake.com/blog
www.artstreamstudios.com